There Is No Good Time
for Bad News

Aruni Kashyap

FUTURECYCLE PRESS
www.futurecycle.org

Cover photo by Aruni Kashyap; cover and interior book design by Diane Kistner; Georgia text with Effloresce titling

Library of Congress Control Number: 2020949163

Published by FutureCycle Press
Athens, Georgia, USA

ISBN 978-1-952593-06-2

For Dr. Dipti Dutta Das,
who used to edit my poetry.

Contents

titles & subtitles that indicate an assemblage, collective, family shared experience

Alpha Ursae Minoris

From Ranjit Singh's diary, October 1962

It didn't feel like defeat until we reached
the foothills, at the end of the City of Love,
where a castle surrounded by fire
protected the princess thousands of
years ago, to be crossed only by the man
who would marry her. It didn't feel like a retreat
though we had cringed like earthworms
exposed to sunlight, like a snail that twitches
under a drizzle of salt, a catfish that
is stunned by a blow on its head. It
didn't feel like that because we were
mechanically marching downhill, without
boots, with wounds on our knees, our frostbitten
thumbs numb, heels cracked like
the chests of fields after a long drought.
It didn't hit me until we saw the people
with bags of clothes, crying
children, tense faces of men, red eyes
of women. Ahead,

the city unspooled like our souls:
buildings on fire, schools converted into
refugee camps, thousands of patients from
the halfway house staggering about. We
didn't want to show our faces to our families,
these people who made sweaters for us, women
who took off their ornaments for war funds.

We abandoned our uniforms, pulled
our hair, laughed uncontrollably, merged
with the madhouse patients,
asked passersby: *What is the function
of washermen in a country of nudes?* We

awkward cadence produces discomfort, a feeling of un-reality

> surprising analogies

Ranjit Singh = 19th century maharaja & ruler of Seikh Pakistan

Rife with subtext I can only begin to guess at, showing me how much I don't know about this culture & historical event

are ginger vendors,
and yet we need to know

about

lighthouses,
Orion,
the North Star,
and the routes of sailors.

The Prime Minister's Visit

[handwritten: → juxtaposed w/ maharaja's diary]

As the crowd swelled, dust
flew in the air like shredded
silk-cotton in windy
February noons. People jostled
smelling like lime, coconut water;

[handwritten: ⟩ visceral immersion in senses.]

by noon, they smelled like rotten lime; underarms
covered shirts, blouses, darkened
by sweat, dust, anticipation, fatigue, journeys.

Our family had used a bullock cart, though the
people in the village said it'd be wrong
not to walk to watch a great man, who was
almost godly. Housewives twittered like sparrows.
Putting on their flowery blouses, hanging earrings,
they chattered about the last time they had gone to Sonapur.
Grandma's mother-in-law described his long nose, wondering
aloud if he could smell flowers blooming in distant hills
or the perfume of dust-darkened underarms, had read
all the books in the wooden almirah eroded by termites.

[handwritten: personification]

[handwritten: → connection to smell]

It was difficult to get in. A young girl
vomited at the entrance. Security
looked on while her mother slapped her
for spoiling her silk dress, her trip, her
opportunity to see the long-nosed, god-like man.

[handwritten: → juxtaposition w/ reality]

Many of them could see only his long nose,
while almost everyone saw his cap:
white. My grandma, who
was a young bashful woman then,
saw his hand only, about which
she talked for years, sometimes
laughing, sometimes
with bitterness.

[handwritten: ⟩ white cap?]

My Grandmother Tells Me About
the Earthquake of 1950

[handwritten: → connection to nature]

First it was just the ants;
like water bubbles, blood
that oozes out of a wound, they
emerged from their holes carrying grains of rice.
We thought it was because
of the impatient slanting rains that must have
percolated, flooded their bedrooms, dining rooms, living rooms.

[handwritten: animals as warning]

But soon, even though it wasn't the season of
fleeing birds, the birds left their nests; angry crows flew from
one tree to another, as if one of their own
had been killed. But they just cawed like frightened people:
didn't try to claw our cheeks,
pierce our eyes, as if
they were trying to tell us the secret
knowledge of the ants, alert us as they always did
about uninvited guests. One evening,

[handwritten: → superstition or reality]

the wild ducks, the
sparrows, the kingfishers, the woodpeckers left noisily:
empty nests with eggs, nude beehives
that hung from large branches dripping
golden honey in the sun, forming puddles below with no ants
to drown in sticky sweetness. It was

then we knew something was coming,
though we didn't expect it would be the river,
because we'd come to this village fleeing the furies of another river
that attacked paddy fields, houses, and swept away
brothers, sisters, mothers, lovers, concubines. On the day

it came—August 15, 1950—we were planning to gather at the
school playground to sing the anthem, distribute sweets; but I fell
down while tying a bun, and I thought a dacoit had entered, pushed me,
to take away my gold necklace. I couldn't stand up, and the rattling walls

told me to crawl out, screaming for your grandfather; the courtyard
    was slimy
with thousands of earthworms germinating from the soft soil, while
water from the hot spring that had sprouted
in our courtyard burned my cheeks; one of my legs
stuck in a deep crack. When the trees shook their heads,

we didn't know about the newborn river that had sprouted
from the chest of a nearby mountain; → *bigger picture*
we didn't know it was one million times
stronger than a bomb called Fat Man; → *historical context*
we didn't know that the creator of
Fat Man and Little Boy had looked at the test explosion
and recited a chant from the Gita — ?
Now I am become Death, the destroyer of worlds.
Even without you, every warrior in the enemy camp will cease to be.
But the ants and the birds
and the howling dogs and foxes knew,

so
they left,
so they howled,
barked.

Fake Boots

I

We found her lying under the bed, a machete
clutched in her hands, drawn with love
towards her breast, as if to fight the whole world
of alien Hindi words, stamping feet and a camp
of green-men near the river where women no longer
bathed, after many women were stripped.

She must have thought,

> she would be one of them now
> who were peeled to be enjoyed by many;
> for hours since, she dared to speak silently to walls,
> cicadas, four puppies huddled around a milk-heavy bitch.

> Maybe she thought she would be one of those
> who came back with his crushed testicles to wail for nights
> like hernia patients while their wives burned
> forever on beds, fearing opinions and wobbling tongues,
> though there was nothing as such to crush in her—

> perhaps only squeeze, though they were dry
> and hung like weaver-birds' nests
> from coconut branches in loamy soils.

She had been sleeping, the crumpled bed said; the hot-water bag
her earning city-son brought from the concrete-jungle slept
instead of her on the bed. When I sat on it, exasperated,
it was still warm with fear, comfort and urine.

II

We were only playing *military-military*.
Carpet grasses had just started growing from our groins.
We couldn't smoke if we wanted to, or watch films in cheap halls,
join the United Liberation Front if we wanted, the way we can now.

But still, those were better than days when
we sneaked behind tamarind trees
and sang *Bihu* couplets to girls, who had just learned
to wrap a piece of cloth around their chests and giggled,
poking each other in secret parts.

We had new shoes that night; the
neglected *Durga*-idols waited
to be immersed in rivers and we thought—
one night, eating peanuts, *jalebis,* and *besan-pakodas*—
to knock at my aunt's door while she slept with
the puppies, the walls and the heavy yet trying-to-be-warm air
inside, where she was left alone to wait for us
who pretended to wear boots, speak Hindi

and ask about the ULFA.

*Reality vs.
make believe

child vs. adult

innocence vs. knowledge
(and fear)*

No One Would Hear Me If I Screamed

I had expected to see
vendors with colorful sweaters. Though
it was late January, it was still the season
when you wanted to stay longer in bed, under
the warmth of the quilt. The night before I had
to push my husband away from the fire he had lit
in an old black iron cauldron that was missing a handle
on one side. I told him to go sleep
(my hands cold, wrinkled after washing the dishes)
because we would have to start early tomorrow, catch the bus, grab a
seat before they were filled up with dirty men and women
who went to sell ducks and vegetables in the city,
who didn't mind waking up early,
who went to bed early despite warm crackling fires.

The cold would stay on
for a few more weeks, if not a month,

I had told him. So we would have to find
those vendors, though we were actually
making the trip to the city to buy golden silk for
next month's wedding.

But I didn't see what I had expected to see.
Instead of the children
who should have been roaming with tiny
flags tucked in their shirt pockets,
I only saw people running. A group of
clean-shaven young boys came sprinting, shouting,
asking the people to shut the shops. We ducked
when someone threw stones;
Something must've happened
during the Independence Day parade, he said.

We took shelter in a small
gully, where no one would hear

me if I screamed. But
I didn't know

who would come for rescue,
who would take away everything that I had,
though I knew it wouldn't be the ornaments
or the money only.

Pressed against the brick wall
like a child playing hide and seek, I
heard my heart echoing the pounding steps.
People screamed. Shops rattled
shut. When we crawled out,
I saw hundreds of strewn slippers. *They should
leave our state, they aren't locals,* an officer told us. *This is the den of
those parasites that suck our blood,* my brother-in-law told my husband,
while his wife shook her head, agreeing. Later,

she showed me the posters she had made by staying up all night,
along with her son, his friends, her husband, her husband's friends.
I didn't ask her where they would go,
why our people, the locals,
couldn't set up businesses, do better.
Why terrorize people
who were working harder than we were,

we who loved to sleep late,
work less, earn more,
eat well, reluctant to move out
of the state in search of jobs?
I was a newlywed bride; propriety gagged me, just
the way conscience was gagged by emotions in
the subsequent years.

The House With a Thousand Novels

This is a house, L-shaped,
seven-hands high; soil-veranda—
with twenty-one novels in it.

Every evening, five daughters beyond the banks,
who rested like bees in other houses,
with higher, lower or equal soil-verandas
and more or fewer novels,
lift a night-black iron cauldron
so that it squats on the hearth.

This is a house with twenty-one novels,
forever spanning in episodic form,
like long yarns.

       In the room facing the east, where the eldest son lived,
       an almirah stood, with termites battling against it—
       every night, along with the odious I'll-take-you-away song
       of the bespectacled inauspicious barn-owl;
       proud, filled to the neck with a thousand books.

       Many of them were novels:

popular, unpopular, pulp,
erotic (hidden between old "important" newspaper cuttings).

This is a house with eight doors,
seventeen windows, no ventilators.

In summers, heavy with sweat and skin,
snakes creep in for coconut-water-cold soil,
coated cool with greenish cow-dung,
the epidermis of the seven-hand high veranda.

Every day someone comes in,
leaving rippling traces forever
like generational earthquakes:

A wailing woman leaves a story of
oppression,
licensed rape, barrenness, adultery;
a married daughter, beyond the banks,
comes back to disrupt diaries;
a worker runs away, digging up hidden gold jewelry
from one of these story-ridden rooms.
This is a house
with a thousand serialized novels
floating in the heavy air.

Someone shrieks every day.
Someone reads the caws of the crow and expects guests,
picks up a mosquito from the milk and prays that no one dies,
lights a mustard-oil lamp in the household's prayer-room
singing pleading songs.
And children carry love letters for peanuts from here, from there,
leaving traces of story
to be ruminated forever:

with meals.

At night, around winter-fires,
the chewing and grinding of betel-nuts,
while lifting the iron cauldron.

This is a house with a thousand novels
(or more).
Every window or a room that mourns for a vent
treasures a story in it, which
no worker can run away with—
more precious than gold
buried deep enough, deeper than a spring, a well,
so that it lives forever and grows
like tears, hair and serialized novels in journals—

inadequate to live anymore
in a wooden almirah eroded by termites.

The Chinese, Who Came Much Later

The Chinese didn't descend first;
the hill-people preceded them. On the riverbank,
they propped up windowless bamboo huts,
but no toilets.
The cowherds didn't sing about the
behinds of the women who bathed in the river.
They sang about
the Chinese, who came much later.
The day they arrived, the riverbank swarmed
with people like ants on sugar cubes, empty ships a rarity.
An old man told the young ones that bundles
of currencies in the Tezpur Reserve Bank
were tossed into flames.
Those young men vanished the next day, perhaps in search
of those fires that sometimes acquired green flames while
burning the pictures of Nehru, Gandhi. And, still,
the cowherds didn't sing about them, nor
about the schoolteacher who described the holiday trip
of the vacationing Prime Minister
or the women who knitted sweaters
before the Chinese eventually came,
before the flames took a green hue that some young men
had gone in search of. They braved
the marauding army
just like those people who tried to leave
on boats, waited at the riverbank
like ants forming a ball
when caught in a flood.
The cowherds were concerned
about other things: skins of women
who had come from the hills and lived
in houses without toilets, Assamese women
who would be picked up by the Chinese.
They were worried the fair-fair ones

would be picked up by the tiny-legged Chinese,
the dark-dark ones
left for them to marry. On the day
the Chinese came,
a group of men
ran around pulling out their hair, while
another four showed their penises to
giggling girls standing on porticoes.
Two adolescent boys tore the clothes off
a laughing, jute-haired young woman, fondled her breasts,
pressed them hard when she asked for food, while
a dog barked incessantly like insistent noon-crickets
in the emptied madhouse of the city.

News from Home

News from home comes late to me.
A week or more,
even a month.

If the wind chooses to carry it
against the wishes of the media, the governments,
large dish antennas, transmitters, satellite channel cables chisel it down
so it drops on the way. If you want to know it whole,
you must go back, pick it up like flowers and pebbles
one by one.

But you may not be allowed to furnish it here.
It can have tears, no TRPs.

News from home:

Even couriers reach my place late.
Usually I don't send couriers to my grandmother;
she lives in an antique land of streams, brooks, parrots,
honking geese,
and ducklings (some of them are ugly).

People here,
they tell me these are lands unfamiliar, so I must not speak about them.
I should yearn for a language, which goes well with people who decide
who should know what, how much,
how many times, when, in which perspective
and how many days news from home
should take to reach where I live,
so that tears dry up, hence no TRPs.

August

Here, August is the deadliest month.
On rail-tracks, amidst forests, green paddy fields,
trains halt overnight like gigantic caterpillars,
waiting for safe passage. An aaita says, *Why do people like*
to travel inside a string of matchboxes?

August could be the bloodiest month—
in some summers, we have seen corpses carried away
on biers, like slaughtered mutton hung
in meat shops—*How much per kg?*
As if the army waits for a man carrying
a jute-bag to approach.

Last week, we traveled at midnight
through the forests of one-horned rhinos.
The chill shivered us to the bones,
but we were eager to smell the forest,
had decided to wait, in case an elephant stood
on national highway thirty-seven.

On our way back the next day,
we saw footwear strewn across the roads,
burning buses, cracked cars, and a woman
crying, with a split skull—they had pelted her with stones.
Worried, she asks with the suddenness of winter rain—
Where are my car keys?
The drugs for my asthmatic son?

Far away from the capitol, a village
decides to celebrate Independence Day
by unfurling black flags, just like
the days when the Union Jack fluttered
from police stations, courts, offices.

At Age Eleven, My Friend Tells Me
Not to Wear Polyester Shirts

I really don't know why you still share
your lunchbox with him, because he belongs to the other tribe
and he hates us now; but until yesterday he used
to love us quite a bit because he had come
to my birthday party with a pencil box, though
my aunt had sniffed, saying that a pencil box
didn't cost too much. I had liked it so much,
we had sat down together beside my sister's harmonium,
drawn Mickey mice on plain sheets, and Ma had
called cheerfully when she found us with those pictures
     for everyone to

come see, come come see

but I was so embarrassed because
his Mickey was better than mine, with the ears done very
sharply; my Minnie was bad, too; instead of looking like Minnie,
she had looked like Mickey, like a Mickey who is sad just like
the way my mother sits sad these days after a hand came flying
onto the roof of our grandma's village because the tribals like
him have started hating us; when his mother met my mother
at the marketplace, she wore a *dokhona,* spoke to my mother
     in Hindi
when my mother asked her questions in Assamese. I have watched
many Hindi movies you know, *Mainey Pyar Kiya* and all, so
     I wanted

to correct her Hindi, tell her that she wasn't making sense,
     but I didn't say
anything because our driver had told me that they would
     throw bombs
on our roofs; I couldn't risk that. You shouldn't talk to him
     because
he hates you, talks to you only in English, that strange Hindi.

Haven't you heard
about the buses that went up in flames in Rangia last
        month?
The car bomb that went off at the marketplace in Kokrajhar
        last week?

I saw the photos when Ma fed me cucumber salad:
Burnt flesh turns red
when your face comes near fire, clothes stick to you. You
should never wear polyester.

There Is No Good Time for Bad News

I

This is the thirty-second time she
has come to identify a body. This time,
I am sure it belongs to her son. In his pocket,
there is a bloodstained letter for her, and
another written to his lover who isn't
here anymore; she teaches in a college in the city,
probably married.

We aren't responsible
for informing everyone. We will only inform
the next of kin: his mother. His father

died long ago, of natural causes, but
of course, everyone in the village
knows that he would have lived longer if he
hadn't had to change sides on the bed forever
after the cruelty of bayonets on his body that had forced him to
do frog-jumps in front of his students across
a large field.

I am sure it is her son's body,

I knew him, too. When we were young, we planned
to join the same militant group because
we were so inspired by the man who came with
a satchel to talk to the villagers. We were young;
we were at the cusp of adulthood, still angry
about those eight-hundred-something protesters

who were shot dead.

II

When his mother comes to identify the body, you
will have to make sure the women from
the village flank her like trees beside a road.

Like her previous visits to identify bodies, she
will crumble like a house of cards,
throw her hands up to the sky like
ascetics who feel betrayed after years of penance,
bleat like a goat that feels
the sharp edge of a knife against its neck,
scream like a woman in labor.

You have to hold her
tight like a perp trying to escape, you have to
tell her to be patient like trees, make sure, when
you reach her house, there are enough women police who
can hold her in case she starts
running on the streets again

like a lunatic escaping from an asylum.

III

It was nineteen years ago,
the first time I went to inform:

> *There's a body that matches your son's description. Someone
> from the family must come.*

Baba!
  she had gasped
  and fainted, though I didn't tell her

that forty-nine bullets were pumped into that body. His father
was alive; the counter-insurgency operations
hadn't begun with the aggression of overflooded rivers.
When she was awake, pale like a bed of grass after days

under a brick, she started to run on the coal tar road,
screaming *Baba, Baba,* her long clothes trailing her like a tail.
Baba! On that hot summer day, molten tar on the road
gave her blisters, sticking on her feet like a bad reputation;
for weeks and for months I carried those regrets
like a daily wage-laborer's task, because
it was the wrong body. It

didn't have the dark leaf on
the right side of his neck.

Baba! Baba! Baba!

IV

In a country where bodies of young men pile up
like trash in landfills of large cities, we
need names attached to them like tags that hang from plants
preserved in botanical gardens; we need

mothers to identify birthmarks, fathers to sign papers, brothers
to carry them on their soldiers. Parents of insurgents
are always the first on our lists. They deserve
the first chance to say
No, he doesn't have a black leaf
on the right side of his neck,
where is the mole on his upper lip,
where is the birthmark on
his left thigh? Bodies with broken bones,

bruised
battered
bluish
bitter

faces.

V

Now,
I have chai and samosas
while preparing the inventory: a diary,

a notebook with phone numbers from China,
Bangladesh, Pakistan, and other enemy countries;
four rounds of bullets, an AK-47, antibiotics,
letterheads with rising suns as watermarks.

Every year,
the number of bodies I see
are thousands and it doesn't
matter when I deliver the news. There is no
good time for bad news.

VI

That's why when I had to ask the same family
again to identify the sixth body that matched
her son's description, her Baba's description,
I didn't think twice before delivering the news though it was

the day of her second son's wedding: He was in his white dhoti,
smeared in turmeric and black pulses paste, with a jasmine
garland around his head. I whispered to the father but
the mother knew, because mothers always know,
and like all five previous visits, she ran howling, wailing;
we ran after her, the village women ran after her,
the groom ran with water dripping from his body,
turmeric paste, foam from Cinthol soap

but couldn't catch her before she collapsed on
the road, exhausted, like a marathon runner, with fast breaths. *Please
forgive me,* I told the brother, who still smelled of fresh turmeric. *Please
forgive me, it is my duty to inform every time
the description matches,* I told an exhausted father.

VII

In the evening, the fireflies bloomed
in the air like tiny floating stars; the stars
shivered, crickets sang, the day I went to inform
her for the eleventh time. Her second son had left the

village, unable to stand the pain of hammered needles
on the tips of his fingers and nails, lost for answers
about a brother he had met almost a decade ago, who went

in search of a sunrise, when his family shivered
in the brutality of winter. That was the year his father
had started to stare for
long hours at the trees, skies, walls.

There was a group of women on the courtyard,
dehusking golden rice grains, when I stepped
out of my jeep to deliver the news: *There's
no good time for bad news,*
I told myself again. I waited for her wails
to cool down. I waited
for the women to revive her
by massaging coconut oil and water
into her scalp,
squeeze a lemon on her scalp,
make her smell things.

Someone gave her a ride in an auto-rickshaw
while the others walked
like a procession towards the police station.

At the gate, she said, *I can't
do this*; bleated.
At the door, she banged her head thrice,

*I can't do this,
I hope it is not him.*

At home, the father stared at the sky,
counted ants,
talked to the dogs, cows;
tried to catch crows and
climbed under the bed in search of
female mosquitoes.

VIII

But this time, I am sure, it is her son. How can I not
identify the man who advised me to gift orchids to
the girl who is now the mother of my children? The man

with whom I played football using a large elephant-apple
because we couldn't afford to buy a real one? I knew
him before he left for Burma, before he decided
to make a home in the forests of Bhutan, before
he decided to abduct Russian engineers and
Indian social workers, before he started talking about Indian
spies, before he wanted to live in a country that still exists in hope.

Listen, I want the local clinic's doctor here.
Listen, I want more family members here.
Listen, I want the doctor to bring first-aid;
this is the thirty-second body she will come to identify.
This is it. She will never come again.
Listen, send the police station's jeep—

she shouldn't walk all the way.

IX

Outside the precinct, a large number of people have
gathered. *I don't want any trouble*, I tell them, *no slogans. I only*

want his mother to be taken care of. She
is alone in that house she wouldn't move from
because, if she changed the address, he wouldn't

be able to find her. She must have been out. Now she is wearing
clean clothes, isn't running, isn't screaming, isn't falling apart.

I want to hold her hand and tell her,

Cry, this is it; he has come
back. You will never have to set foot in this police station again
with a heart that beats like a scared duck's wings
and examine the wrinkles on battered bluish bodies with
bitter faces.

Wail, this is your son,
I have seen the dark leaf on
the right side of his neck and,
unlike other bodies, this body is intact,
the face is intact, the skin isn't burnt,
the eyes aren't eaten away
by wild rats and ants.

I want to hold her, say, *I am here, cry*
as much as you want, but she goes in,

doesn't cover her nose
though the smell of blood and the body
like rotting lime and rice
is strong. She presses her palm

across his forehead, holds my hand,
and says,

it is him,
this blood on the floor is my blood,
this body on the desk is my flesh

but she doesn't cry, she doesn't wail. She
walks out

with the calmness of a saint,
bright like burnt gold.

My Aunt Talks About Being Raped By Soldiers

My husband...

had never put it in my mouth before
because...
I had never imagined it could even be put
in such places. At sixteen when I eloped,
clutching the collected coins that I had wrapped in a hanky after
breaking
my earthen piggy-bank shaped like an elephant, I carried nothing
but the cotton clothes I had on,
the notebook where I used to note down
teasing-songs so that we could sing those at weddings
to irritate grooms who came from faraway villages
on carts drawn by tall hornless bulls.

My man was gentle with me.
On our wedding night, he took time to slide himself into me,
asked me again and again if I was okay; stopped whenever
something oozed out of my mouth: a sound, a muffled yes or no,
a long breath. Unlike the other women of our riverine village—
women with whom I sat munching chopped olives
dressed in rock salt under the sun
during breezy late fall months—I never had tales
of strange positions; so I had fainted

I had
fainted

fainted; when they
took his body away for cremation,
I pulled at the fully bloomed red rose plant
in front of our courtyard,
uprooted it in one go
until my palm and the roses were of the same color,
until the women had screamed that I had gone mad,
that I would faint,

that my blood pressure would reach my head,
that no cold water on the scalp,
no coconut oil on the hair,
on the forehead,
would bring me back to life

but

it was only just that moment
when I had lost control.

I wanted to live
for the smile of my two-year-old son,
for my four-year-old daughter,
for the thirteen-year-old son who had just started
to be a little distant from me,
who had just started to have broader shoulders
than he'd had two years ago;

there was still time left for his shoulders to broaden up slowly
like an inflated balloon, like the moon that moves
from the sickle-moon night to the full-moon night
in fifteen days; there was still time
for his voice to wear a new skin
like snakes changing the upper layer of their bodies after
a certain age to gain new skin. I knew would have to live
        for them,
without the gentle touch of the man I loved
who asked me if it hurt,
caressed my hairy groin with his rough farmer hands
before slipping into me;
who never asked me to put it into his mouth;
who left me alone during those months when
I told my children that I was
hiding a pumpkin under my sari.

But this man in green clothes
who had come with a gun
asked me to do things to him
I had never done to my husband—
if I did, he would leave
my ten-year-old daughter alone.

I am so thankful my son wasn't around.
He was sent away to his uncle's house
after his father's death for a better life and education.
I am so thankful the officer didn't kill me, unlike
the other women in the village who were left to die by
other soldiers and officers. He was a high-ranking officer
with soldiers around him who waited outside
when he came every alternate day after dinner

until it had become my habit to wait for him,
until it had become my habit to put the children away to sleep
after cooking early on the hearth so that
I could go to sleep after the regular ordeal,
until it had become my habit to stop resisting.

I always burned the notes
he slipped between my breasts before dressing,
before walking away. I don't know if you have seen
burning bills, but it looks good when notes
burn in green flames; and please note this down, too,
that he paid me though I didn't ask; write about this also in
        your report
so that everyone knows; I can't believe
I have to narrate such things to an unknown man,

but please do write everything
on your paper's front page
along with my picture.

Where the Sun Rises

Letter from a girl to her insurgent lover

If you come back,
there will be no sun,
like the day when we met for the last time in your room
and there were no rains, only thunder and stars.
    ARSD hostel, wasn't it? There was no sun,
    but we spoke about the next day's sun
    that would gaze at its face in the mirror called the
        Red River.

If Brahma hadn't married and Parashuram
hadn't killed his mother,
this river, the mirror of the rising sun,
would have remained tumultuous, caged,
like this heart today, in the Parashuram Kunda, forever.

If you have a mother and a father
who still earns and orders, you can't bathe there.
If you bathe there, all sins are washed away
like peace, as after the sun rose in Assam in a green flag.

Parashuram bathed there, and like blood his ax descended,
but, still, he is the mother-killer.
Parashuram, there is blood on your hands—
your mother's.

If you come back,
what will you bring?
the Red River is redder now.

During independence, Rupkonwar sang a song,
jingoistic, nationalistic: *We aren't scared of sacrificing our lives;*
we will make the Brahmaputra red with our blood.
On the altar we will lay our necks,
even if the priest runs away terrified.

What will you bring?
Those days are no more,
those days when young Assamese men sang so that the Whites
would go away,
sang so that more young men would come and join the processions.

Green was there, even in that flag,
and if there was blood in 1947, there is still.
The Luit has become redder; that's the only difference.

I don't know what happened in Burma's forests.
Did you bathe in the Lake of No Return?
What will you bring for me, if you come at all—
mosquitoes, malaria, wounds and jaundice?
Or hunger for flesh and food to the point
where flesh will be food and food will be flesh?
      Flesh will be food and food will be flesh.
      Flesh and food.
Nobody will cook for you
nor for me. Flesh and food are the same now.

A redder river weeps, not for you
but for peace and a natural sunrise,
yearns for redness from the sun floating between clouds,
not on a green flag.

How I Felt a Week After My Son Left to Join the Militant Organization

Something feels wrong constantly. The switchboard
creaks like wrought wood doors
in abandoned houses of kings
flanked by tamarind, jackfruit,
Banyan, and mango trees. Bathroom-water trickles down like
the slow unfolding of a story, as if someone is there.
Something is wrong. *Something is going to happen.*
I can hear the mouse screeching wickedly: Do mice screech like
a car coming to a sudden halt? That was not the only unusual part.

My heart skips so much; it flaps like a headless hen dripping blood,
spreading dust through its refusing-to-die wings.
The dust settles on me like sediments and
refuse to leave. I sweat,
go breathless, feel cold. I think I will faint.

Dear India: A Collage Poem

for Allen Ginsberg

Dear India, what kind of an idea are you? Do you
bend at all? Do you sway at all, trimming
your bluish shades? Why are you
proud of a 50-year-old shame?

Dear India, please do not forget the sweaters
women in Assam had knitted,
the ornaments they had donated; and do not forget
that James Bond has killed 150 men and
has slept with 44 women since
the first movie came out in 1962. That is
also an important matter.

Dear India, there were few boats that night,
when people were fleeing Tezpur, feeling
betrayed after they'd heard the vacationing Prime Minister's speech.

Dear India, please wake up.
Have some strong Assam tea (Korongoni will do but
I love Golaghat Tea, too—you can get it in small
250-gram packets if you don't want to spend a lot)
and stop glorifying 1962, as it is not the only story.

Dear India, have you read *A Single Man,*
Christopher Isherwood's novel
set in November 1962, about a gay man in LA? Have
you heard of the book? How about the Cuban Missile Crisis?
You know, I am a great fan of Lata Mangeshkar. I think she is super cool.

Dear India,
In 1962, an American Airlines Boeing 707 crashed on takeoff
at New York International Airport after a rudder malfunction
caused a roll, resulting in loss of control of the aircraft
and the loss of all life on board—there are other
stories; please read some at least, India.

Dear India, go fuck yourself with your atom bomb,
with your commonwealth games,
with your T-3 airport.

Dear India,
you need an education.
Dear India, why do you make me
feel ashamed so often? As if seizing the virginities
of fourteen-year-olds by Indian soldiers in the '90s
wasn't enough.

Dear India, please pack
your bags and go to school. It is getting late;
your Assam tea will not remain hot forever.

Dear India, you might
just miss the bus—have you done your homework?
Madam will make you kneel down in front of the class if it is incomplete.
Please do not stick your arms and legs out of the windows of the bus,
and better finish your tiffin today, including the bananas.

The Militant's Mother: A Letter

After Ezra Pound and Hem Barua

Moromor Baba, here, I have just lit the candle
to write to you after a very long time. Moromor Baba,
we had so many hopes heaped
on you: You will do well, ace the exams, go to
Cotton College to study, become an Indian
Administrative Officer and return home
with cars with red lights and sirens that would
wake the village from stupor. Your father startles
at night. He hasn't forgotten how the officer
asked him to frog-jump in front of his students for
raising you, hasn't forgotten
how he wasn't allowed to wear his dhoti. After it slipped down,
he frog-jumped forty times in his underwear from one end
of the field to the other, until he reached the silk-cotton tree;
and when the women moved their faces away and his students looked
down at their own feet, the officer shot a dog and screamed: *Look,
look at him, look look, look at him!* But, Baba, if you come, if you
come once, he would forget that pain. He would move his hands
over your soft hair and say, *Ahili? What will you eat? What will you
eat, Baba?*

Baba, we love you—don't doubt it. We know that you have
read more books, have thought about the world more
than us, but I want to see you once more. I want to know if
you are eating well, if you have lost weight. Please come
once again, so that I can look at your face to say, *Ahili?* I will
serve your favorite *payas,* with lots of cinnamon. I will
cook your favorite fish-tenga, with fewer green chilies.
Don't avoid visiting us—do come.

Even if someone informs the officer, we want you here.
Your aunt hung herself from the large jackfruit tree after
the officer touched her, Baba. Your brother left for the city
after they hammered sharp pins in his fingertips because

he couldn't tell them where you live, what is
your next plan.

Remember that silk-cotton tree at the end of village? Last month,
a strong bolt of lightning burned it down. Now
it is covered by a yellow parasitic plant.
The village elders say it is not a good sign. I am
worried it means it would take longer
for you to come. Remember

the dog that was shot dead? I have adopted her two puppies,
now seven years old; they guard our house. They don't know
how their mother was killed—only I know, only your father knows, only
the village knows—but the river that carries the reflection of
the sky, it knows everything, including how your father
who stares at the skies most of the day feels.

PS: Baba, please come. Send news with the milkman or the fish seller,
like you usually do. When the fish seller brings a bunch of boriola fish
and suggests cooking it with mustard, I know what he means. I promise
you, when you are coming down from the Tamulidobha River, I will walk
up to its bank to receive you—as far as Ghoramara, where the horse died.

There's Nothing to Worry About

I thought about that story my friend told me over phone
when the bomb exploded in my hometown.
I was too busy to get
through to my mother's phone,
because she goes out to buy groceries during the evenings,
when office-goers return home on scooters, on buses, in expensive cars,
clouds of smoke following them like haunted pasts. She doesn't
listen to me when I ask her not to walk on
the uneven pavements of the city,
though she has stumbled several times,
though she was taken to a nearby pharmacy
once with a bleeding nose;
after one of those torrential monsoon rains,
she had stepped into a manhole and had to be pulled out by
  five passersby.

I had barred her from walking outside our
protected campus from then on—
the campus where yellow-black birds chirp
during spring. But, soon, she had defied my instructions
because she didn't like the clipped freedom within
the four walls of the protected campus. She
liked to check out the jewelry on the street,
chat about diseases with old women,
discuss the behavior of new students
  with former retired colleagues.

So I was worried when Google told me there was a new blast,
and when I heard her voice; she asked me not to worry,
because she hadn't gone out yet with her jute-bag
to get groceries,
  to check the roadside stalls where
  vendors sold jewelry,
  to walk on the manholed pavements where
  she met former colleagues

to chat about the behavior of today's students
who
spoke to teachers while chewing bubblegum and paan masala.

No, I didn't think about
that story my friend had told me when
Ma said,
There's nothing to worry about,
because the bomb exploded four kilometers away, in Ganeshguri,
and only fifteen people have died. Chandamari is
a different market, and most of the bombs,
after all, are planted only in Ganeshguri because it is
close to the capital complex. I pleaded with her to stay home,

wait it out, because you never know if they
have planted a series of bombs, but she said
Saikiani would be waiting for her because
they had been planning to have Irish-cream coffee
at the new restaurant, then visit the new beauty parlor
to check out rates; and though she had hung up, holding
the phone against my ear I thought of the
man who was returning home in a dictatorial state, where
there were shoot-on-sight orders if people were found on the streets
after ten, and how a security guard randomly shot him; when asked,
the guard replied, *He's my neighbor, he wouldn't have reached home*
    before ten.

Spring 1979

I

I never met them to exchange
polite meaningless words,
never sat with them and debated over
cups of strong tea boiled with ginger.

But I have met them in my dreams
after sniffing them from dusty newsprints,
from talks with my father, with whom
I had gone to find a rare flower
once, but could never hold it.
We just came back, exchanging
polite meaningless words with
the men who he grew up with,
with whom he played football
with an elephant-apple; men
who looked eighty at fifty
on whose chests you could
play the harmonium soundlessly.

It wasn't my metaphor.
Father told me, in the forests when we were
returning, making way by trampling German-shrubs,
exchanging meaningless words,
that some flowers were lost forever,
that it happened when a terrible beauty was born.

II

Grandma told me they went in search of a sunrise
across the hills, crossing rivers, brooks, fields
to come back withered, with wounds on their hands,
with hollow hearts where sounds echoed; she doubted
if they would ever sleep again, especially

that boy, who was picked up because he had a
copy of *Das Kapital* on his table that he had borrowed
from the school library, his sight sucked away
by the brightness of five-hundred-watt bulbs.
That boy doesn't even wear shades;
days and nights are the same for him.
It happened because a terrible beauty was born.

III

Sometimes at midnight, I have heard the wails of seven
strange women; in dreams I have seen fourteen bleeding thighs.
Someone tells me: Like the teeth-imprints on their necks,
scratches on their breasts, those rivers of blood
aren't from their thighs; you should be able to
read in the dark, find meanings, smell beauty
even in the coldest winters, hottest summers.
With brass pots hung from their necks, with
jute ropes around their necks, they bid the world goodbye.
After the night when the sounds of boots entered their homes
a few years after, a terrible beauty was born.

IV

I have only heard about that woman
who returns every month, sometimes even twice,
from the morgue with the smell of corpses
stuck to her nostrils, clothes and hands,
and only because she wants to know if one of those
is her son who took a whole sky away with him
when he merged with the forests; in that house,
all alone, she sings about the days she walked on the streets
when a terrible beauty was born.

V

We also snatched small skies with us, carried stories
thousands of kilometers away. Some of those
stories will be told, for we believed not in the power
of stories but in the power of ruminations,
congregating, speaking in the language
of pain and ecstasy, though we are away
from the Red River, the hills that give birth to rains also.

The Red River? Who hasn't written a poem for it?
Who hasn't thought of it when we saw the Thames,
the Mississippi? Who hasn't missed its redness,
its whirlpools and mystery, even on the banks
of Yangtze, Jiang, or Hudson?

But one day we all shall come back, with different stories
this time, with a belief in the river's power
to transform pain into joy during censored times,
learning to ignore the sound of boots: rendering
them insignificant, unimportant, invisible just
with the power of a hopeful story of revolution

or maybe a song

and a terrible beauty to be born.

An Invitation to Murder Me

It is very easy to kill me. Every morning,
I go for a walk. I walk through the perimeter
of the thousand-year-old rectangular pond, where lovers
sit or jump every evening. The Handique Girls' College
is always to my right. At the turn, I reach the entrance
of the pond again. To go ahead, I take another turn in front
of the state museum. To reach my small apartment next
to the pond, face the High Court and turn right.

My apartment is small. There isn't much protection
either. Before sleeping, I lock my door with a Godrej lock. It
is rusted, time-worn, from the days of my grandmother. A single
blow with a rock or a hammer would destroy it with a thud, spreading
rust on the floor. You can break in; and if you
let me know early, I will leave the door open. You
don't even have to spend a bullet on me; no need
to plant a time bomb. Just press a pillow on my face; I will
stop breathing. To kill me, you don't have to go
all the way to the upper reaches of the river. To kill me,
you won't need a bomb. I hoist the national flag
every year on Independence Day, though the nation gives me
reason to be ashamed every day. So

you should
target me,

not

little kids

who go to Independence Day
with the hope of eating sweets,
        because
they love to sing patriotic songs
without knowing their meaning,
        because Independence Day

is a holiday for them. Their little limbs, burnt skin,
     severed
heads as small as the dolls they carried,
     are
still on the grass. Instead of killing
     more babies,
please come kill me. I am
     an ordinary
person; I use an old lock
     in an old apartment to protect myself
from the invasion of hatred. You will not need
     bombs; you
will not need guns, bullets; you will

just need a pillow.

Diary Entries

Param Singh

The first time my father said we starved him
for five days, we thought he was joking. My mother
burst into laughter, asking
what was wrong with him. It was
his creased forehead—which we were all scared of—that told us
he meant what he spoke, he believed
what he said.

Ranjit Singh

And one day, it snowed at the barracks. There
was nothing left to eat. I had sent a group of men
to kill bison, goats, crows, pigeons; they returned with the carcasses
of wild water buffaloes. Major Sahab said
that he sent wireless
messages to the camps down below, and that when
the Prime Minister returned from his vacation,
things would shift like weather: food on our plates,
sweaters to wear, more woolens at night. The
wood wouldn't emit smoke smarting
our eyes. We will not have to roast the water buffalo
carcasses on a spit. It was
before one of my tent-mates
vomited all day after eating
strange leaves for breakfast, and another left behind
a stream of blood on the snow as he walked. *The Chinese
are coming, the Chinese are coming*, Major Saab
murmured in his feverish state, shivering near a fire.

Nishita Singh

I wasn't even married then. I was still living in Jersey,
going to school, almost living in archives when Param
phoned me that Father had started to forget things. My
father, who remembered even the color of the frock
I wore when I went to watch *Chitty Chitty Bang Bang,*
who remembered what mistakes I made during my
last test, now can't remember what he ate an hour ago,
our last names, first names of neighbors. When Aunty Farheen
visited us with sevai on Eid, he asked her who she was. She
cried, *Ki bolcho, I am your sister Dada, I am your sister from
Bangladesh, Dada; if no one feeds you, I will
never let you go hungry, Dada.*

Sujata Singh

I didn't tell the children about those sleepless nights
before he forgot about his meals. I wanted to
handle him on my own; when he kicked the air,
punched the pillows, woke up with a sweating body, I
screamed *Hai-ram* before jumping on him and pressing
his shivering wet body against the mattress
that was hot and wet, sticky, nauseating.

1962 Again

In Manhattan, I become instant friends
with a young man at a bar who tells me about his father.
What are the odds? I ask, and laugh.
Param Singh and I complain about
Grindr Boys and the weather, drink beer.
He is British, US-raised since he was an undergrad,
lives in the Bronx, still loves to take
long walks across Manhattan. *What*

are the odds? he asks, laughs too, though we are
far different from each other by age, by likes, by preferences.
He invites me home, because after all, what are
the odds of us meeting here, in this city? Days
later, he tells me about a black woman he married for a green card,
a lover who returned to India, his desire to return to India,
meet his grandparents, and walk on the soil of the
state that his father refused to talk about. I told

him it has hills, rivers, rains, tribes, stones the size
of lizard/duck/pigeon eggs smooth like babies' bottoms,
bison, occasional snow, Buddhist gompas. Thoughtful,
he takes a walk across his room. The carpet is blue,
not Turkish, but feels Indian-India; I am bad with designs.
My father, my father, he said, *lost the thumb from*
his right hand there. We were meant to meet,
he says. He sounds American, British, desi.

During the last days, nothing
would stop my father from feeling cold: the blankets in June,
the heating turned on in May. Shivering,
weeping, screaming in horror, he collected all his coats,
sweaters, to give to his friends who were dying of
frostbite. We had to tie him to the bed, and he
died a caged animal. Behind him,
the Param Vir Chakra stares at me
from a red wall. There is little light reaching

the room from the tall buildings in the Bronx. Sounds
of sirens. Fire trucks. Car exhaust. Singing people.

A bronze medal for shivering in the New York summer,
for leaving the country, for finding another profession
in Britain. Far away from the state of rains, tribes,
bison—but what are the odds that, even in faraway
New York, the winter wouldn't stop chasing him?

The Man Who Loved to Plant Water Spinach

The man who told us to plant water spinach
to stop the river came from far away. He
wore brown leather shoes, checked shirts, torn blue jeans,
and no hat in the breezy summer of the river island.

The sound of bell metal and devotional songs
welcomed him. Women admired the blue veins
on his neck, gifted him cotton *gamusas,* hoping
he would pluck orchids for them, but

he was just interested in the river, in planting
water spinach. Old women who had lost their
gold and husbands in floods, children orphaned by waves,
and Muslims who had to throw their loved

ones into the river since there was no place
to bury the dead, embraced him as one of their
own, started loving him more than those men
who carried guns, stopped the production of
local liquor, punished roadside Romeos

by making them hold their ears in public or
smear soot from the bottom of large cauldrons
on their faces. That's what the gun-loving moralists didn't like:
Why was he interested in stopping the river? Why
did he plant water spinach? They

didn't believe that he wasn't an Indian spy. One
dawn, they tied his hands and carried
him away from the shrinking island he loved
so much. When they pushed him, he

transformed into a turtle that loved porridge and
paddled into the unreachable parts of the river. Until noon they
searched; in the distant land he came from, his wife fed rice to
crows. For months there was no news of him. Years later,

one of those young girls who was orphaned by
the river met a large old wise turtle with torn jeans
wrapped around its body. *When they catch me,*
chop my limbs before I am killed, the turtle said. *Let*

the village feast on me. You plant my flippers in four
different corners of the island, and I will protect
it by covering it in the form of water spinach.

Freedom

After Paul Éluard and Birinchi Bhattacharya

Freedom, we are still waiting
to paint your name on the hand looms
that weave red flowers into cream-white silk,
on the emerald meadows sprawled
dreamily in the blue sky's embrace.

Freedom, we are still waiting for that ship
to arrive with your name inscribed on its mast.
We still believe your name will be
painted in cheerful blue on its sails,
which will flutter in the air
like the hair of a village girl
in February—when red flowers bloom
like mischievous ideas in a child's mind.

Freedom, we couldn't write your name
on banana leaves with blue fountain pens,
on grains of white rice with needlepoints,
on the echo of our childhoods,
on the fine surface of rice husk,
on the transparent wings of dragonflies,
on their pink-blue-green tails.

Women couldn't melt you, shape you, stud you with gems
to hang from their soft earlobes; men
couldn't wrap you in strips of newsprint,
like tobacco, light one end, take a drag,
recline dreamily against tree-trunks
on summer noons. Children couldn't
peel you like ripe mangoes. No, you couldn't
even be the walking-stick of grey-haired ones or
a drop of water on their tongue before
the final breath.

We couldn't usher you in.
We couldn't make
you sit on wooden dining tables, serve you
an elaborate meal though we waited so long
with our doors ajar, clothes washed,
verandas mopped with fragrant water,
or with cow-dung blended with white soil
brought from the riverbanks.

But here, on the wide banks of the Brahmaputra,
you were defined everywhere:
on the ruddy rivers
where, instead of fishes,
chopped limbs stuck in the nets of fishermen.
Where fingers with and without nails were
scooped up by a woman who went to wash dishes
in the stream that ran beside her house.

Often freedom was written
between the legs of women
left bleeding; on the penises of men
who only spewed white froth
from their mouths, not information.

Freedom, we are still waiting
for your arrival. Until then
you will be performed
and explained, because ancient stories
tell us: Definitions have always
belonged to the definers.

Notes

In 1979, the Northeast Indian state of Assam burst into an armed insurgency, demanding to secede. Like other lesser-known insurgencies in the world, this conflict between the Indian state and the rebels, along with the stories of people who suffered, went largely unreported. During this period, more than thirty thousand people were killed on both sides; many more were injured, handicapped, and killed extrajudicially by the Indian army. These poems take a look at this violent period and reflect on the consequences of prolonged violence on people. Revisiting India's birth as a modern democracy, zooming through wars, protest marches, and conflicts, the poems tell us what it meant for me, my community, and the common people to live under the scourge of violence. Told in voices of people who suffered (mostly women), they introduce the reader to a wide array of characters: soldiers suffering from post-traumatic stress disorder, grandmothers who recollect historical events, housewives who share mundane events of a day, women who talk about sexual abuse, and mothers mourning their sons. Invoking Indian folk songs and the poetry of Allen Ginsberg, Ezra Pound, and W. B. Yeats, the poems take the reader through a journey from the remote and underrepresented regions of India's Northeast to the streets of Manhattan, introducing a wide array of characters who are unable to escape the experience of intergenerational trauma perpetrated by the State.

—A. K.